These Few Seeds

Also by Meghan Sterling

How We Drift (chapbook)

These Few Seeds

Meghan Sterling

Terrapin Books

Terrapin Books
4 Midvale Avenue
West Caldwell, NJ 07006

www.terrapinbooks.com

ISBN: 978-1-947896-39-0
Library of Congress Control Number: 2020952060

First Edition

Cover art:
Snowmelt by Betty Schopmeyer
oil on wood panel, 24" by 18"
www.Bettyschopmeyerart.com

This collection would not have been possible
without the support of my husband, Matthew,
and the existence of my daughter, Adeline,
who inspire me daily to love more and be better.

Contents

One

Morning Prayer

It is the beginning. It is the beginning
when there was you. It is the beginning when there
was you and me and her, before it all just became life,
when it was new. Can you remember?
We are there now, again,
standing at the beginning where we can hold
the new of her, the new of who we had just become,
our new names. Mother. Father.
Taking these names from our ancestors,
all the others who were what we are now,
taking these names out of the air
before we have a chance to try them on.
Our new names. Standing at the edge of water,
praying for our daughter's safety.
It is the beginning when there was you and me and her
and the water that's rising—
oceans, lakes, rivers, streams,
all rising on this morning
still soft with the night that was just here.

Sidekick

It was along the beach, always, that great revealer
of the secret body, ungainly as marine life. We were
dolphins caught in a rip-tide. We were beached jellyfish.
We were a pod of seals spread across the sand,
shining like puddles with their grease rainbows.
Barefoot, feet a little sticky. Hands also. Snap bracelets,
scrunchies. The walking and walking. Through hidden thickets:
Indian hawthorn, lantana, rosemary, sea rocket, woody goldenrod,
pennywort. The paths littered with flecks of metal, paper, condoms
like shrapnel after sex, and we were ancient, wise as wild horses,
weaving our way through our habitat when the boys would come
and we would bend, we would weaken. We would break ranks.
Flocking to them. Hungry, aware of our bodies being appraised.

I learned my art: the blade that slices, that separates skin from bone,
the way one path forges another.

Say you forgive me. Poison dart tongue. Face a mask.
Machine gun smile. *Rat-a-tat-tat*. Clumsy joint passed
beneath the palmettos. Say you understood the ruse.
Be the clothespin. The mother in her white pinafore
and hat like a basket of flowers. Be the wildflower meadow.
Creator of the hot air balloon. Psychic. Reader of palms.
Superhero's sidekick. Walking along the yellow beach,
grasp the knife handle plunged deep into the wet sand.
Be surprised when it slides out easily, your mouth a mottled O
shining in the rusted blade. Be a killer, sexual adventuress,
librarian with buttoned neck and glasses and no panties.
Holster the knife, keep walking—there's a group of boys
lounging ahead, boys who love a good story.

California

is always coming apart somewhere, a fire
or a fault in the earth opening
itself in love, in ruin, which is to say
utterly. This place. Eucalyptus
in wide stands filtering light and exhaust,
leaves like wings, the ocean eating
the side of the whole state, like it can't get
enough of those shore pines, shards of cliff
jutting out into the Pacific.
After all, *California is a poem,*
Steinbeck said, and like many things, he knew,
he saw the truth. This place can break you.
Cherry flames ripping up the sides of whole mountains,
redwood forests ringed in mist.

Camera Lucida

We were in love then. Early winter,
the alleys like paper scraps of snow.
Seeking each venue as if the next reading
could deliver salvation.
I wrote on scraps,
refusing to show the others,
letting those scraps grow damp between fingers,
pushing them against the seams of satin pocket liners.

In the alleys, we smoked Marlboros,
shaking in our acrylic gloves, in coats with too-short arms.
We quoted Kafka, pretended we had read everything.
You carried a small suitcase with journals, pencils,
sharpeners, a protractor—you wore your eccentricity
as an accessory. Without money for meals, we ate at bodegas,
saved our pennies for museums, for jazz.

You stole your books from the Strand.
We went for long walks in Park Slope,
looking into windows lit with abundance,
dreaming of living better than
boxes on the stairwell, found furniture.
Everything smelling of last week's cooking.

At night, we huddled on the mattress,
read passages from Barthes' *Camera Lucida*,
shared joints rolled from the cheapest shake.
But poverty wore, frayed like our sleeves.
You stayed out later, I started reading English novels.

Your father offered you a salary
to study business, and when spring came,
you tossed your suitcase out the window
into the muddy alley, your papers soaring
like white birds.

Still Life with Snow

It fell away, that slant of light
that followed us across the North Sea,
across a stable yard, hoofmarks
sunk into the frozen mud. The way the barn
cut the night in two, the hay steaming,
the chickens asleep in the roost. I had dreamt
us before we ever came to be, clutching the cold
like a talisman against the bruising of old dreams,
against the inevitable age that would grip us
in its fulsome mouth. A dog in the yard
mawing its one mean bone. And what sky was left
was hollowed moon and piecemeal as a memory
of what I thought I could be if only love would
find me, traveling the Arctic of my heart,
gnawing its white bone.

Memory is a Greek island

twisted in the red dust, blue anemones,
gray olives, green figs, keeled over
in Aegean winds.
Here I declared my love of open spaces.
Snapshot of hair blown into sculpture
after a day of walking.
Snapshot of moonlight on the sea,
still cold from remembering winter.
Snapshot of six nuns in blue habits laughing
in the bed of a new pickup truck careening
over the rocky trail down to Parikia.
Every village a different arrangement of white stone,
blue doors and blue sky, sky that swallowed all sound into itself
like a church. We were still friends then,
before we fell into too much space.
Here, the wind blew salt over the fields of rock
and we learned the plants like a new language:
dianthus, lantana, kite flower,
as we climbed the hill to see the ships
come into the harbor.
I decided here to love all that I was given,
no matter how much it hurt.

Adeline

In our house, we always have dusty window frames,
glass jars of tea, loose scree on the walkway.
Lately, too, small evidences of her,
sounds of sleep, quiet breathing
soft as moss on stone, the dim roar
of the monitor, a small sock wedged beneath
a door. Agony of any distance.
Even in the next room, I dream of her
behind my eyes, my belly still holding memory,
the sky stripped of cloud,
her perfect breath always in earshot,
a weathervane, right as rain.
Insistent, a dripping tap, running
in a rust line down to a drain.
In our house, she is near as my cells,
in the woodgrain of floorboards,
cradle of smooth gray walls.

Man Subdues Terrorist with Narwhal Tusk on London Bridge

It's another day, and I am in a mostly clean bathtub
enjoying quiet in the lavender-scented water
when you knock on the door—
Did you hear about the terrorist attack on London Bridge?
A man subdued the attacker with a narwhal tusk!
and chuckling, you leave, letting that fill the room.
I lie back. The occasional drip of the tap as the scene unfolds.
A crowded afternoon. Brilliant blue sky. Sudden screams,
a man charging another with a narwhal tusk.
Steel railing of the bridge, November air. People scattering,
the chaos of extraordinary situations. Smoke from a fire extinguisher,
nothing in focus except the tusk like a white light a man lunges with,
an unwieldy foil. I imagine the feel of it in my hands,
ivory helix, spots of decay, 5 feet long and 22 pounds.

Did you know, the original bridge is actually
out in Arizona somewhere? I say to no one in the quiet bathroom,
the water cooling. But I remember London Bridge.
I was 20 and looking over dizzy into the water,
people rushing behind me. London always busy.
All the lives lived hustling, trying to survive cold winters
over this bridge, over the Thames rough with winds,
hands cupping candles in fingerless gloves, or selling matchsticks,
and I remember a handsome young man in a white blazer
nervously smiling at me as he rested against the railing,
and I have thought about him on occasion for the last 20 years,
as if he were a gem I was searching for
but hadn't the courage to pluck out of the stream.
And I remember crossing bridges without fear
of smiling men or terrorists or knives,

passing by narwhal tusks mounted on the wall
of the Fishmongers Hall without registering them
as possible weapons. Probable ones.

O, the innocence of 1999,
when London Bridge was just a way for us to cross the water
between the City of London and Southwark.

Cyclops

I have always loved like this: one eye in the center
of a face. My mother's eye, bloodshot on a September

afternoon. My face gray with the growing cloudcover,
late summer storm. And yes, I have loved the eye

that looked away, with one eye shaded by the raised fist.
I have loved the eye that didn't see, the eye that saw me naked,

or claimed it had. The eye that loved my shape, then spit
in the chalkline of my body, leaving me its gun.

I have loved my daughter's prizefighter face,
one eye swollen shut with the effort of being born.

I have loved the finger that jabbed the eye into darkness,
the hand that slapped the eye shut, the hand that nursed it,

the mouth that sang it into sight. I have loved the eye,
black, brown, blue, gray, green, nearsighted,

myopic and strained, near tears and distant,
watching the sun, desiring blindness. And I have loved the eye

in the mirror less, but it is always that eye
I am seeking.

Molokini Crater

The way desire could wind around
me like a cat around my legs,
a purr loud enough to drown the no
right out of my mouth, the soft fur of it
scratching, tripping me up.
He never once asked if I was happy,
and when he asked me to become his wife
the NO inside frightened me into a small yes.
And while I lied and the too large ring was floating
towards me over the clear water,
I saw the birds of paradise, stiff and orange,
splayed like flaming wings wide to the sky
above the nearby cliff, and I wished I were braver,
a bird of paradise—alone and arcing,
not this false bride afraid to wrest myself
from the lie of my life, afraid of the backlash.
Which happened, and soon, stripping me nearly down to bone,
but not that day; that day was cool blue ocean,
sharks slow swimming beneath us,
a too-large ring, a terrible fear,
the false smile which confused the photographers,
and that premonition of doom.

Two

Jew(ish)

In our home, small traces, only: the menorah
in the cupboard, a mezuzah in a drawer.
notes from my bat mitzvah in a book,
a mizpah ring in a box on a shelf.

The word carries, though, a series of sensations:
weight of the ornate silver, of long lives and sore feet,
and the sound of plastic taken off couches
for the Bris, for the Seder, for the Shiva

when the clothes are cast out of closets in a hurry
as if the dead would come back for their pants
if they were left. And it's a quality of air,
like cigar smoke, but thinner, and the warp and weft

of woven blue and gold where the weaving is tangled
in the back. And the sweet purple in the throat
of Manischewitz and the tongue coated with egg and crumbs,
and the smell of hair oil and of paraffin just after a candle

has been extinguished, and the color of the circles under
all of my family's eyes, and the yellowing pages of books
with the corners crumbling into dust, and the dust
of all the dead and the smoke like ghosts in the streets

that shame us into naming ourselves, outing ourselves,
to keep them from disappearing.

Marfa, TX

In the desert, the sky is low,
snake-belly white to the ground and blurred
with unnamed stars like a face after crying.
I arrived there with a broken tent and toothpick legs,
standing in a town square with tumbleweed
and Wallace Shawn like a desert garden gnome.
All travel leads us to the same conclusion—
how alike we are—
even me and Wallace Shawn, standing in an empty town square
under a sky yawning with clouds like giant chrysanthemums,
our mouths taking water from Marfa's pipes and cisterns,
our yearnings an echo,
our faces the flesh of the local cactus.
Never has the wind been so loud,
the sky screaming with its bright blue
crying like a bird of prey above a bell tower.
Never has the sound of the wind been so like the sound
my mouth would make if I could speak
to Wallace Shawn,
telling him something memorable
while the tumbleweed circle us like hawks.

Daughter

I dream that the earth is on fire beneath us—
that is what love is. I take you
into myself as though you are the petal
pink to the open hand, a plum stone sweet.

And what was broken opens wide,
all the things I never knew or felt in an explosion
that feels like pain, but is fear and a terrible hunger
to save all this for you to live in,
an ocean that asks for tenderness,
a sky that begs for quiet.

The waves of your soft hair
are all that stills the thrashing of a heart
that's been submerged and drowned
a million times over.

I need you to be safe,
your face already a memory,
as though the smoke from a burn pile
has created its sepia tone.

Notes on Domesticity

Bright wind, a space inside,
empty like an O-shaped mouth.
Too soft, the way the air moves
easily between us, fingers wide
against the sun, a delicate shell pink
at the webbing, moving filament,
moving the white curtains above the bed.
A nearness, without curiosity, without dread,
a long time bending, like wet wood,
the heart's chiming bell, and now, after years,
letting each other pass in the hallway.
Your body distantly, distinctly scented,
sheets wrapped around a thigh,
or water running behind a bathroom door,
the way spaces between rooms
give us permission to keep ourselves away.

All That I Have Is Yours

Somewhere in the field I heard a voice
tell me to make you. Maybe it was the creek
winding through the clumps of mown hay,
or the finches shaking the redbud branches
with their small wings, or my heart urging
me to do something good, something I hadn't
known if I could, with bomb-crater hands,
with shot-shell chest.
                My hope still winter-numb,
flinching at touch. But I saw at the edge of the creek
my face grown small,
remembering near voice, morning light slanting
across warm skin. And I broke apart
and turned you into being, choosing
to go as I had gone before, but braver.

The Absence of Birds

after the painting The Village of Monhegan, Maine
by Emil James Bisttram

What was missing? The cloud movement
above a delicate line of rooftops, poised
as if in flight. A bird that wasn't there.
Was that it? For a moment,
I was nearer myself than skin, than touch.
I knew the bird as it flew invisible,
a blue stroke behind cloud. I felt the truth of light
as it spun down from a distant sun.
The absence of birds, and the truth of what it is
to be sitting barefoot in a gallery
avoiding the guards,
this moment connecting me to the girl I was
at the Met, when I knew my life was hidden
in the streaks of paint, and I walked around galleries
struck with sudden knowing.
Twenty years later, sitting at another
birdless sky and I the bird. No nearer light,
and yet, the blues that carve
their crags into the mountains, I feel them
under my hair. The mountain's veins run with the blood
before me and after, and I for a moment get to see it.
Maybe this blood is what beauty is.
Maybe if I were a bird I would know fewer but deeper truths:
the feel of air beneath me, the small adjustments
to allow carriage by wind.

Asterism

Rigel, Aldebaran, Capella, Procyon,
Sirius, Castor and Pollux,
hexagon of light tonight, its winter pattern
just above trees in an oak's crook,
like quilted indigo, white stitching.

It shines in the snow that ribbons up
the trees' wide arms after a winter storm,
which is how we love each other:
gently removing her hand clinging to my breast,
in the silent way our feet touch the floor
to avoid the creaking board, in the way
we whisper once she has fallen into
her exhausted sleep, all the lights
in the house dim but for starlight
that pricks dark windows like needles in cloth.
All this is belonging as I've learned it.

Quiet, near—an evening sky violet with snowfall.
And in the hours that she sleeps, our daughter
breathes with her face turned full to the sky,
lit as if the stars had found her tonight
like the night she entered the world
when the rare snow covered the town in silence,
the stars showing their fullest brightness,
as if the very fabric of space was in awe.

Where We Can Be Wildflowers

Come to a place where everything is clean—
mind, kitchen countertops, towels sparkling,
starched white, all white. Everything white
like we are royalty or live in Boca Raton or Texas
or California with its ocean rolling up against cliffs,
vaulted ceilings and horses. Wide expanses of wildflowers
with nothing to do but seed the air in soft tufts
and flower where they land.

Come to a place of acceptance—dirty clothes, mildew,
fungus under the bathroom sink, dishes sticky with ketchup.
Countertops the color of mud, like the streets of the Kalitsky shtetl,
the hems of my great-grandmother's one dress. Dream of the home
we will build when we can save some money—cut out pictures
from magazines, paste on a board to look at when the apartment
feels too small: claw foot tub, skylights, white kitchen sink,
new wood floors that will feel secure, staked, bolted to the ground.
Dream of the garden—wheelbarrow full of black earth, field
of pink flowers that means you own land, you till land, you work land,
which your grandmother in her one dress could never do.

Come to a place of forgiving—the flowers nod their bright heads.
Stories your grandmother would not tell are not your stories.
Her village is not your village. That mud is not your mud.
These countertops are temporary. This field of wildflowers
lives inside you because your memory of her demands it.

Monster in the Water

Every day, I go down to the water.
If I kneel there long enough,
maybe I will become the water,
ribboning as it flows,
like the dance I learned as a girl
where by whirling fast enough,
no monster could reach me.
And even if the monster is the water,
as it rises, as it warms,
not of its own doing, but of ours,
if we make of it the monster that we are,
as we make everything in our image,
if we become the water
before it becomes us,
maybe we save something of it
in ourselves, the silk of water
as it rushes over our skin,
the shine of water smooth
beneath moonlight, the sad, slow
wash of water as it runs
towards an ocean that's rising, rising.

Three

Queens

We choose one way or another. Or we are chosen.
Is there a difference? The shadow, it wears us.
Your mother, scrubbed clean. My mother, drowning.
The mothers they became, clean and drowning.
We become our mothers, shadow of them grown long,
cast from an open door onto the bedroom floor.
Quilts hung over footboards. Endless solitaire.
Words swallowed like food between more bites of food.

Patience, patience—your time will come.

Mother still as well water at the table while her shadow
eats and eats, full to the brim, water edging just above the lip.
Shadow of water I wish would pour onto the dining room floor,
filling the house, never spilling over.

The Queen card damp, not finding its way into the piles.
The Queen card sitting off to the left.
Her jewels in a box beneath houseplants,
water rings white on brown wood.

I remember after a night drinking
when I thought I could tell her what I knew.
That knowing burned into my skin like a signature
shakily soldered into soft pine.
What I learned: the truth can catch fire,
the truth only belongs to those who learn its name.

We don't become our mothers unless we choose to.
Their shadows dealt and scattered, should we pick them up,
try to place them in piles, should we back away, and even then,

they live in our handbags, beneath the folds of the bedsheets.
They live whether given food and water, or just air, like orchids.

Remind me that I will be different.
That I will speak because I am full of words,
a stream of words, and because I am not
stopped, plugged, choked, blocked or bolted.
Remind me that water is meant to run.

Center Line Rumble Strip

The lake water looks like skin, a long line
of smooth, dark skin I hunger for,
alone in this cabin, where I pretend its creaks
are a voice telling me something illicit.
Long nights, late mornings, dew beginning
to frost the webs on the porch:
I don't have time for delicate things.
I want to dive into the lake to cool off this heat,
the mist clearing quickly like an angry arm
sweeping the dishes off the table.
I feel the two fronts meeting—
the autumn air cool as the heat of me rises
each day you aren't here, steam
sputtering off my skin like an iron left on,
the car cutting to the center of the road
as it stumbles on the yellow strips that buzz it awake:
a seatbelt digging into my chest, memory of touch,
memory of hours around us like clouds
before there were 3, when we could slip easily
into connection, sleeping like doves in the eaves,
heads under wings, or startled into rising
when our hands or feet would touch from parallel solitudes.
Now, without touch or voice, each sound
knocks me into presence, into truth.

Puddle Jumping

It's so brief, her small hand
reaching for mine, reflexively
as if my hand grew out of the earth
wherever she is and needs steadying—
as if my hand were bannister,
tree branch, root.
We ready ourselves:
ladybug rainboots
with the big gash in the rubber,
flowered raincoat just now too short in the arms.
She dashes forward on unsteady legs
seeking the puddles as if thirst drove her.
The biggest one gathers at the grate
flecked with orange dirt
like iron rust that glows beneath the rushing.
She wants me near her, to delight with her,
to exclaim that this puddle is big,
this puddle is dirty,
this puddle is cold,
as she stumbles, she splashes,
she seeks my hand in the air.

How Many Times

And just as suddenly, as though his ghost had more weight
than his body did, he is back. In the messages being left.

In the sleepless nights, memories I can't shake.
How much is required to feign indifference,

as if I hadn't loved fiercely; as if I hadn't come to hate
fiercely too. The secret life that beckoned him

with its bone-white finger got him at last,
but I had already grieved, torn my clothes, beaten my breast.

My grandmother used to scream when she heard of a death,
three times without passion, as if it kept more death away.

When I heard the news, I felt as if I were an empty bell being rung
hollow and deep, carried across distant water.

How many times can we mourn a death?
Again and again, yes. But never like the first.

Retreat

To sleep in a bed alone after
five years of marriage
is a practice in restraint.

Pillows like the spines of leaves
still clinging to the branch,
the sway of wind that tries to knock them loose,
or more like doesn't try at all, just moves
and things blow, settling into skin
that only I can touch.

I'm trying not to love the room too much—
the lamplight, the mattress leaning to the right,
the blankets wrapped around my selfish legs,
a smell of soap and mint,
my spacious thoughts clean as a plate,
and no cry from my daughter's crib
to jar me from dreams
of fallen branch, single stone.

Siren Song

Whether the pines stay stubborn
or lose all their needles, and the maples

never again bloom into flame, marking time,
or we don't find lady's slippers deep in woods

to keep secret and untouched,
or a grassy spot for a playhouse

or a treehouse and a garden for our daughter,
and we don't find a well dug fresh and deep

to cool our mouths after days of working,
or we don't build four walls and a roof to keep the rain out,

and if the ocean rises to meet us all with its cold kiss
while the coast breaks off into it in small pieces,

and even if we have to crawl or take a wagon train to the backwoods,
we have to escape the sirens along Brighton Avenue.

The Deeper We Dig

First Layer
The truth looks more like my grandmother's face
every day I am alive. The mirrors know it. They show me
what's real: my own face becoming worn, trenched, where hers was.
And though I run and run, in cars, planes, trains, feet on the ground,
I always end up in the same place, with stories,
and the ones I lift out to live I've lived before.

Second Layer
I dream I am my grandmother, her face looking back at me
in the train car window, the train rushing into a mountain
in Ukrainia, a place we fled before the first World War,
with the Anna Karenina train cars, with the Slavic language
emanating from a cut throat,
flurries over a wide field, novel left open on the blood red seat,
pages growing wet with snow.

Third Layer
I have seen what we will become when the ground opens up,
our skin the metal of machinery. I dream I am the truth
as I look into her dead face in mirrors, in windows
smeared with hair oil, the way the truth I say isn't the truth you hear,
but lives behind it, around it, evading,
the passengers all imagining the past they see out the windows
is the future.

Tit for Tat

I got the news the same day
I started dreaming him again.
Ghost-eyed, hungry, in last night's dream
he paraded by a plate glass window without his pants,
his legs marked by the tracks the needle left
as he hunted me. I had turned my back after he turned his,
after he had made his choice on the living room couch.
When his death brought him back, I saw a difference—
sadder, sterner, desiring things I could never provide.
Do you have it? he charged last night,
as I tried to shut the front door on his arm, reaching,
reaching out to punish me for loving him once, for promising
to give myself to him. *Tit for tat*, my grandmother would say.
You make your bed and you lie in it. And I lie in this one,
dreaming again and again,
of the long dark hair like a veil in front of his face,
and how much he hated everything I did
to try to make him feel.

Excavation

Exactly where were you
when you decided to hide?

There were palms along the Abada,
jasmine in the streets of Damascus,

white like stars in the night after a bomb
makes its transmutation.

All the longing as the cobbled dark tripped you
on your way to your hostel,

as the men gathered into mountain ranges,
as the women collected themselves into hijabs

and became the new moon.
You weren't as invisible.

You could witness, and be witnessed,
an obvious assortment of limbs.

You turned your face
to the sky bright with pollution

when a prayer made itself into
the song, *Stay hidden. Stay hidden. Amen.*

Once on a plane you found a paper scrap
with your father's handwriting:

loving for a lifetime is no small thing,
again, witness: years of holding an angry dawn,

strangers sharing space, the stories
mothers keep inside their eyes

like the women in Damascus,
their faces behind the burka.

If only every woman in the world could choose
to reveal or hide, phases of the moon

compelled to alter as the mood demands.
We have only begun to claim ourselves.

Upon Hearing the U.N.'s Report That One Million Animal and Plant Species Are at Risk of Extinction Due to Climate Change and Human Activity

Winter comes later, and the grass
never fills in the front yard,
small brown rings like a pox.
After nights of heavy sky and heat,
cows and dogs bow low
as if weather carried weight.
We watch our daughter,
painted white with zinc
in rough grass, make believe she is a cow
and laugh up the dying trees.
Pretends now she is a squirrel
she remembers from *The Tale of Squirrel Nutkin*,
laughs into the echo.
She gathers and piles dried oak leaves,
threads them together in the crumbling crown
she places on my head.

Codicil

To you, my daughter,
whose earth may not be my earth,
whose earth may be scorched
with flames,
whose earth may be ripped
apart by gunfire and blood,
whose earth may wilt
under the heat of a too-near sun,
whose earth may reveal her
ocean beds to be desert skin,
whose earth may be hardened with
sand and rock,
whose earth may wither
dry as a peach stone,
whose earth may be divided
by walls and colors,
whose earth may be sunk
with pills and powders,
whose earth may thunder
with the rattling of trucks,
whose earth may be
sour with salt,
whose earth may be
drowned in melt,
to you I bequeath
all the courage
of birds and flowers,
water and stones,
to love enough,
to love with the toughness of trees.

Four

Mincha, Afternoon Prayer, Meaning "Present"

the rabbi says, bowing his head
and raising his hands to the day
as dust shines in a beam onto the chalice
he holds, light angling across the backs
of men trying to stay awake,
nudged by their wives, their children
swatting each other,
knocking a prayer book to the ground,
and as we fidget in our seats, trying to connect
with God, the sun glints through the windows
of the synagogue like God's provocation, as if to say
I dare you to love, I dare you to live despite this suffering.
Can you? Can we? We can love this light, this sun,
however brief, our sun, just one among countless stars
that soften into galaxies, showing us that to die
can be more lovely than to live,
that the shell of us will decorate the sky
for eons to come, and be more beautiful for it.

Weaning

No longer cleaving, your black and white shape
in the infrared light, monitor box set
on the coffee table as I try to busy myself,
to remember who I was before you were me.

Accustomed to your scent each night,
your body alongside mine, only an arm's length,
your hair, just washed in our bath,
my vigil of putting us both to sleep in each other's arms.

I'm told that this should be a small grief—
so small, like your tender body, the weight of you
scented with powder, grinning into my mouth, your tears
in my mouth, exclaiming the nearness of my breast
in your half-sleep—grasping it with both hands.

It was your sweat on my hands, your drool on my chest,
your mouth opening wide to engulf me,
that is the way I used to feel about love,
which you've revived in me.

What Emerges

Autumn has arrived
with its mute foreboding
as if we, horse-wise and anxious,
could sense the coming quiet
and grow wild with alarm.
Everyone is weeping.
The neighbors scurry
from their cars
to their kitchens
to boil their tears in teapots.
The sun dreams of justice,
shrouded in her weavings,
and there's blood in the veins
of leaves, the way they
keep falling in circles to lie
at the base of the houses.
All the angles have begun
to emerge—chimney-stone,
forgotten bird bath,
the corner of an old receipt
peeking from beneath a pile of ash.
The sky ices over and claims its dead,
culling the rosebush before its buds
have time to blossom and shatter.

TAT II

Under clothing only,
the rationale for inking sorrow into skin.
That it would be shown to those who cared enough
to look, or didn't care at all, lovers or fellow sun worshippers
at the beach. Peacock feathers at my hip,
etched after my grandmother's death,
preferable pain to the tunnel of darkness
of New England winters, before my daughter became
all my sun. Now, like a sports team, like tropical birds,
we wear our feathers in unison, and she touches them, fascinated,
in the bath, or while we wrestle and my shirt comes up a bit,
the greens and blues streaking up my ribs, or your shirt sleeve
rides up your arm, and the bird is revealed.

I imagine she may want them, too,
since the ones who made her are marked
by an attempt to stay alive, decorated by loss.
She celebrates them with curiosity, this triumph
of our feathers, now that we can see them for what they are:
Freedom. Mistakes. What once symbolized pain
now means survival.
Maybe everything becomes that in time—
stretch marks, scars, wrinkles,
like tattoos, we made our bodies out of canvas
to be new again, for our daughter.

Celestial Event

Still, that song about the star
as if by wishing we can change these things—
these burning forests, these razed forests,
flames ripping across maps
shooting red into the center
of what was once so much green.

But the truth of those colors
is black and white ash, and smoke,
skeletons of villages, a child's toy
scorched in the center of what was her family's bedroom.

Despite the stars that flash above us,
light carved into darkness, the same sky I looked at
when I first saw a winter night,
when the sky is massive enough to allow us to see
where we actually stand in regards to space,
the moon, the Milky Way like a grease smear
on our glasses. A spray of salt across a table.

And only those flickering stars are preserved
from our bulldozers due to their distance—
already dead.

Hiver, Mon Amour

Winter, take me into your arms,
the folds of your white sheets,
long gray lines, pavement shivering,
dark as slate under heavy feet.

Winter, the coffee shop windows
are fogged, I cannot see your steel face,
gaping horizon like teeth.

Winter, hold me wet and stunned,
cover me in flannels, wools, and sheepskins,
gently pressing snowflakes
into the hair that frames my face,
alive and wild in air as dark as water.

Let your ice give shape to my thoughts,
your winds whip my eyes into seeing
what I never do, what I couldn't until you came
and stripped the world naked,
your gaze like judgment,
your touch like stone.

How much I've lost since we first met.
I've been spinning. Keep me still, Winter.
Love me into the hard hard ground.

Bliss

A mountain inside me. A fish.
I never thought I could stomach
giving birth, the very thought!

Still you swam, you whaled my flesh,
stretching the very silt of me
until I was star-marked, blood vessels burst

in a constellation heralding your arrival
across my chest.
All the day before, I felt the sea of you

rock and rock and rock
until the pain began, until you insisted
it was time for me to be more than me.

So you rode your wave out, slowly.
I creaked like an old boat
when you slipped, a just-caught minnow into our hands.

My body then began its deflation
while my heart began to grow big and bright
like the heart in the middle of the page when I write

Mama loves you
and you color it red
with your bold and earnest strokes.

Ferryman

How close I came. The head of a deer
caught in the lights, twinned by the stars
in its eyes in the moment before.

I have killed so many things with my life.
Cows, chickens, pigs, baby ducks,
a cat, a porcupine, a fetus my body couldn't keep.

Accidents, but my hands stink of it.
My vanity. The narrative I tell myself in bed.
My hair curls as a eulogy for all my dead,

unspoken, a rare sunlight sound,
like the breaking of eggs.
My skin grows jaundiced with it,

under the hot lights of the world's quiet end.
I wash and wear it in the soapy cauldron
of the machines that remove our smells.

I have killed a man, too.
It was either him or me
as he tried to drown me with force,

the food
he shoved down our throats
as if fullness could make hate bearable.

How close we were to death then,
our hearts like Charon crossing the Styx,
only to cross back again, but not his.

He was the pole, the boat,
the body with its coin in its mouth,
ready.

Five

Blatta, Genus, Cockroach

I feasted on leavings. Hidden, sorry,
my teeth yearning for the fruit, to taste
what was plainly offered. Could it be

I now refuse to obey the orders
of the long dead? I was shown the full skirts,
the wigs, the chaos drawn like order

in the sand. I spent instead my shiny dimes
on pens and shoes with heels. I, the mute one,
with the fierce sweet tooth, always playing seeds

like a flute between cracked teeth. Hand-holder,
plait-weaver. I have lost my taste for rot.
I have crept like a roach in the darkness

to tell the truth, with these hideous wings,
this coward's heart.

Succession

1

If only we had the sense to fix this.
Small as we are, sharp,
powerless,
like barnacles clinging to the dock
as the water ebbs,
the moon full
on a desert of rock.
It was our hunger
that led us here.
How we grow with our wide mouths,
ready to eat the hull of the ship
that offers safe harbor.
How we crave an ending.

2

Remind me again how we got here—
before the fires threatened,
before our hearts woke up
(finally) at the sight of our daughter,
rising from the ash of our bodies,
soft as the new moon.

3

All things go. The empty bed,
the remains of a meal on the counter,
wood left to rot in the April rains,
bathwater collecting rust.
We can see them again as they once were,
light shining through

midnight trees, when we felt
we were owed something beautiful.
Now we pray for a different phase
to live through.

4

In moonlight, the world.
How we dream the moon
comes closer.
We can show our child pictures—
Flower Moon. Harvest.
Gibbous. Its surface is cold.
There is beauty in where
we are heading.

5

Tell us that it will be alright. Tell us
our small lives can rearrange these
certainties. We open the Tarot.
We chart the moonrise. We consult
the stars. How much we must do
before we can tell our child
that we've left her anything.

Memorial at a Japanese Lilac

I stage my grief,
arranging flowers for something
not imagined,

where your hand brushes the pollen
from my cheek, where your hand
feeds me clover honey.

Everything distances itself.
Your hand, now deep in the dirt
of what once was remains in some form—

your hand. Not dust,
but fingers and skin,
the tips glazed with pollen.

Maybe in death we become a collage
of what we have most longed for—
finally you are roots, seeds, earth:

a bee inside the hive of its birth,
stamen rooted in the eye,
rain that wet your clothes as you sank into mud.

Maybe in death we are most what we were—
the last bee in a field—drinking deep of all the nectar left.

How to Travel Alone

You must be ready for long silences,
trouble finding bathrooms, short, intense attachments
to strangers, the attention of unsavory men.
Bring moleskin to cover blisters, an unlined journal,
pens that won't bleed in shifting cabin pressure,
Tarot cards to guide the journey. Prepare to hear
the stories of other lonely travelers, and grow to love those stories,
use them as if they are your own, begin to forget they aren't yours.
Learn of your grandmother's death while in Helsinki,
grieve along the smooth gray rocks at the shore—
throw stones into the sea and imagine they are piercing
the veil between you. Get invited into a Swedish home for Passover,
encourage British children in a timeshare in Portugal to henna your hair.
Run your fingers through loose bones in a pitch dark catacomb.
Lose yourself in busy cafes and be surprised by who you see
in the mirror. Feel so alone your skin aches. Over quinoa soup,
regale an Australian couple with descriptions of the American North:
wharves, streets caked with ice like ash, the ocean, a bottomless black
all winter. Forget the times you turned away from a shadowed alley,
from an outstretched hand—the times you were afraid.
Let those untaken paths remind you of the choices
that brought you right here, your luggage gathering dust.

A Recognition of Gone

Could I have known better
pines swimming with birdsong

crouching in the margin
where woods met grass

thick tufts of pine needles marking
the border where the wild ends?

Could I have been better
facing the reeds, the voice that left me

that promised it would come back
that never came back, the heart that faltered?

Could I have waited longer?
The shore lined with blueberries

the pond between states like a traitor
your strong back as you paddled

low pink sun drawing you close, a shadow long
on green water, your black curls

cut close like a Roman. Your black curls
smoke billowing from a wood stove.

Little Bombs

The temperature is in the negatives,
so we become weather soldiers,
putting on extra socks, another sweater,
hunch our shoulders to the wind
as we push our bodies towards our cars,
my daughter in my arms, burying her face
in my cold coat, the fabric stiff in the chill.
NPR rings its news in the car—
the protests, acquittals, convictions,
death rates rising, and I remember the Australian fires,
just contained, the hands of the koalas clinging to the shirts
of firefighters, the way my daughter clings to me
when she's afraid.
She and I sing together to warm up.
She likes to change the rhymes—
Minkle, Minkle, Mittle Mar,
and as I join her I see the world
like little bombs in my eyes:
snow, steering wheel, NPR's radio voices,
my daughter's voice, viruses like chorus girls
kicking in unison, fires, the koala's small hands
clutching at us to hold on.

Evening Prayer

Maybe bees remain, pollinate orchards,
ripe fruit for birds that tend their young
and thrive. Maybe forests bind their wounds,
come back fuller and greener from the scorch,
while an evening sky fills, dotted with seeds that land in city streets,
replacing pavement with fields of wildflowers, volunteer greens
for the rabbits, the deer, the groundhogs. Maybe the moon
shifts and tides cover the earth, and coral and whales return,
sharks and dolphins, jellyfish in their see-through pinks
and electric yellows, now unfettered in their access to the blue globe.

Maybe flowers rise, become big and bright and waxy,
hot wet pink and red folds and stamen, pistil and ovary.
Maybe it all becomes still and quiet, the woods silent
but for bird chatter, lakes and rivers
as they rush over rocks, as springs feed them,
while mice and chipmunks, sparrows and swallows,
spiders and nearly-clear bugs with delicate wings
peek out from their meek shadows in safety
when we have gone.

Her Body Bends like a Tent on Fire

Her worth in her body
so they said, and it drummed into her,
entire thoughts cast into the wind
as it feeds fire,
as fire came into the woodlands
that were once wild.
We all were wild then. I remember this—
building a cairn to honor the wood spirit,
building a fire to warm me, sleeping beside it in safety.
The day it shifted like clouds and light
before a storm. Their words—*what is her worth?*
In her body.
Legs. Arms. Face. Breasts. Hair. The body as measure.
Sudden awareness of the body.
Sudden separation of the body from the earth.
How things begin to die. The woods growing dim.
And how long it takes to journey back,
to come together again, body and heart;
the burnt out ends and understory bracken,
too easy to set to light, scattered, dry,
as California rolls with fire,
as the world grieves her losses
as the world and her heart speak
while her body burns.

Apology After the Fire

Worn down, the sea rolls beyond sight,

sand stretches the way a shadow is cast
from rock. The sun an unwanted heat.

We have grown our flowers in the shade of the razed forests,
our faces wrapped in gauze, our hands cupping the water

we save from the occasional rain and muddy stream.
How did we arrive here?

My daughter throws her scraps to the dogs
that wander along highways that once were rivers

that once threaded themselves
through a softening of green.

My daughter knows the meagerness of water,
our constant searching.

But winds, fires, mud, rocks
are in abundance where once there was

grass, bud, butterfly.
I want life to bloom around her the way she blooms

and for her to know the quiet of leaves,
the hum of growing things,

these few seeds I nudge into flower as apology.

Acknowledgments

Grateful acknowledgment is made to the following journals in which some of the poems in this collection first appeared:

Amaryllis Poetry Journal: "Retreat"

The Ekphrastic Review: "The Absence of Birds"

The Eunoia Review: "All That I Have Is Yours," "Blatta, Genus, Cockroach," "California"

Frost Meadow Review: "Bliss," "Celestial Event," "The Deeper We Dig," "Excavation," "Her Body Bends like a Tent on Fire," "Tit for Tat," "TAT II"

Glass Poetry Journal: "Upon Hearing the U.N.'s Report That One Million Animal and Plant Species Are at Risk of Extinction due to Climate Change and Human Activity"

isacoustic: "Apology After the Fire," "*Camera Lucida*"

I-70 Review: "How Many Times" (published as "Hero")

MacQueen's Quinterly: "Cyclops"

One Art: "Molokini Crater"

Rattle: "Man Subdues Terrorist with Narwhal Tusk on London Bridge"

Sky Island Journal: "Daughter"

Third Wednesday: "Ferryman"

"Adeline," "Notes on Domesticity," "Still Life with Snow," "Weaning," and "What Emerges" were published in *Balancing Act 2: Poems by Maine Women* (Littoral Books, 2018).

"Codicil" and "Succession" were published in *A Dangerous New World: Maine Voices on the Climate Crisis* (Littoral Books, 2020).

A big thank-you to Katherine Hagopian-Berry and Eric Steineger for being early readers of this manuscript.

About the Author

Meghan Sterling is co-editor of the anthology, *A Dangerous New World: Maine Voices on the Climate Crisis,* and Associate Poetry Editor of the *Maine Review.* Her work has been published in *Rattle, Balancing Act 2, Glass: A Journal of Poetry, Sky Island Journal, The Ekphrastic Review,* and elsewhere. She has been a Dibner Fellow at the 2020 Black Fly Writer's Retreat and a Hewnoaks Artist Colony Resident in 2019 and 2021. Her chapbook, *How We Drift,* was published by Blue Lyra Press in 2016. She lives in Portland, Maine, with her family. *These Few Seeds* is her debut full-length poetry collection.

www.meghansterling.com

CPSIA information can be obtained
at www.ICGtesting.com
Printed in the USA
BVHW031641060421
604327BV00005B/327